Nutty for Peanuts

By Andra Serlin

CELEBRATION PRESS

Pearson Learning Group

Contents

Get Your Red-Hot
Roasted Peanuts Here!

Your dad says that he's going to make you a sandwich for lunch. What kind of sandwich do you want it to be? Well, for many Americans, a peanut butter sandwich is a popular choice. In fact, the average American eats more than 3 pounds of peanut butter every year. That adds up to about 700 million pounds of peanut butter in all!

Americans eat more than 3 pounds of peanut butter per person every year.

Scientists have traced the peanut back about 3,500 years to its original home in the South American countries of Brazil and Peru. The Incas, an ancient people of Peru, offered wild peanuts to the sun god as part of a religious ceremony.

Historians believe that the peanut traveled a very long way before it finally came to North America. Portuguese traders, explorers, and missionaries in South America most likely brought the peanut back to Spain. From Spain, traders took the peanut to Africa.

Ships carrying enslaved Africans brought peanuts to North America in the 1700s. Peanuts were used as food aboard those ships. The enslaved people later planted peanuts and used them as food.

Peanuts were grown commercially in South Carolina around 1800. At first, peanuts were used mostly as food for animals. However, when the Civil War began and food became scarce, soldiers began eating peanuts.

Children in the 1930s take part in a peanut rolling contest.

In the 1870s, P.T. Barnum was the owner of a popular traveling circus. He began selling hot roasted peanuts at circus performances. As the circus traveled from town to town, people talked about the unusual treat. Soon, hot roasted peanuts were being sold at baseball games and fairs as well as on the streets. A favorite American snack was born!

See How They Grow

A peanut isn't really a nut, even though the word *nut* is in its name. Instead, the peanut belongs to the **legume** family of plants. Other legumes include beans and peas.

While there are four basic kinds of peanuts, they all grow in the same way. The flower is above the ground, and the nut part is below the ground.

After peanut seeds are planted, they grow into green plants with small yellow flowers near the bottom of the plant. Once the flowers have been **pollinated**, the plant begins to send down **pegs** into the soil. These pegs bury themselves in the soil. Then the tips of the pegs develop into peanuts.

Each plant may grow more than 40 peanuts during a planting season. From planting to **harvesting**, the growing cycle of a peanut takes 4 to 5 months.

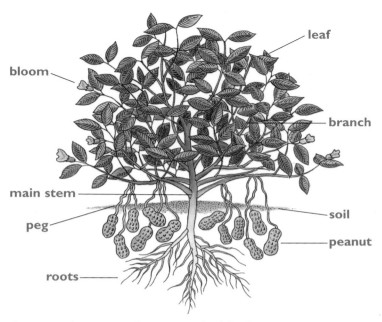

leaf

bloom

branch

main stem

soil

peg

peanut

roots

A peanut plant grows above ground, while the peanut grows below the soil.

The fact that peanuts grow underground is why peanuts are sometimes called groundnuts. Another nickname for peanuts, goobers, comes from the word *nguba*. This is what the Bantu people of Africa call peanuts. During the Civil War, Southern soldiers sang a song about peanuts called "Goober Peas." The song had the words, "Goodness how delicious, eating goober peas!"

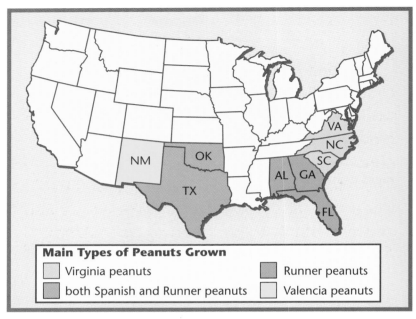

Main Types of Peanuts Grown

☐ Virginia peanuts ■ Runner peanuts

■ both Spanish and Runner peanuts ☐ Valencia peanuts

Nine states grow 99 percent of America's peanuts.

There are four basic types of peanuts. Virginia peanuts are the largest. Because of their size, they are usually roasted and sold as snack peanuts. Medium-sized Runner peanuts are used mainly for peanut butter, although they also find their way into snack foods. Oily Spanish-type peanuts are mostly used in peanut candies. Sweet-tasting Valencias (vah-LEN-see-ahs) are usually roasted and sold in the shell.

Although peanuts are a major crop in the United States, only about 10 percent of the world's peanut crop is grown here. Peanuts are grown around the world in areas with a warm **climate**. In fact, the countries of India and China together grow more than half of the world's production of peanuts. Peanuts are also grown in other Asian countries and in Africa, Australia, and South America.

A peanut seller in northern India, one of the world's major peanut growers

Peanuts are widely grown because they have so many uses. The peanut butter found in 75 percent of American homes is just one way that peanuts are used in food. Peanuts can also be used to make **imitation** milk, cheese, and ice cream that contain many **nutrients**.

Spanish-type peanuts are used to create peanut oil, which is excellent for cooking. The oil is tasteless and can be heated to a very high temperature before it smokes.

Peanuts also appear in many items that are not food. They can be used as ingredients in products as different as shaving cream, ink, makeup, shampoo, and medicine.

There are also hundreds of products that can be made from the shells and skins of peanuts. Paper can be made from peanut skins. Some surprising uses for shells include making fire logs and cat litter!

George Washington Carver

We can thank a scientist named George Washington Carver for finding many of the uses for peanuts today. Carver was born during the Civil War to parents who were enslaved African Americans. Although he gained his freedom as a young child, his life didn't change much. He worked on a farm, gardening and helping with the housework.

A stamp honored the achievements of George Washington Carver.

From an early age, Carver enjoyed gathering and caring for many different plants that were found near his home in Missouri. Because of his knowledge of local plant life, he became known as the "plant doctor."

Since there were no schools near his home that would accept an African American student, George left his home to attend a school in Neosho, Missouri. Even though he was only 11 years old, he had to find a way to support himself while he was in school.

While going to school, George worked very hard. He had many different jobs so he could pay for his education and take care of himself. After he graduated from high school, George's hard work was rewarded. He was admitted to Simpson College in Iowa in 1890. There, George studied piano and art. He enjoyed both, but he was still very interested in plants.

In 1891, he decided to enroll at Iowa State College of Agriculture. He was the first African American student ever accepted there.

George Washington Carver began researching uses for peanuts at the Tuskegee Institute.

Carver worked very hard at Iowa State. He was a great student. He was also a great musician, public speaker, student leader, and artist. Two of his paintings were shown at the 1893 World's Fair in Chicago.

In 1894, Carver graduated from college. He then went back to school to get a more advanced degree. At a time when African Americans had few choices about education, Carver's achievements were very unusual.

After graduation, Carver moved to Alabama to teach at the Tuskegee Institute, an agricultural school for African Americans. Soon, he became interested in ways to improve crops.

Carver began researching the different uses of peanuts in 1914. Over nearly the next 30 years, he invented about 325 different products from peanuts. These included soap, shampoo, cheese, medicine, and ink.

The products Carver created from peanuts and other crops grown in the South helped give Southern farmers a choice of good crops to grow. Peanuts also helped the land. The roots from a peanut plant store **nitrogen**. The nitrogen helps enrich the soil.

George Washington Carver died on January 5, 1943. He received many honors. A monument honoring him was built in his hometown in Missouri. His image appeared on a stamp and a 50-cent coin. Most of all, he helped the peanut become an important crop in the Southern states.

America's Favorite Food: Peanut Butter

Although George Washington Carver invented many uses for peanuts, the most popular use had already been discovered before Carver began his research. A St. Louis doctor developed peanut butter in the 1890s. He used a meat grinder to crush the peanuts. He believed that peanuts would be a nutritious food for people who couldn't chew meat.

Some of the healthy snacks that use peanut butter

Then in 1904, a man named C. H. Sumner introduced peanut butter to the world. He sold $705.11 worth of peanut butter from a stand at the 1904 Universal Exposition in St. Louis, Missouri.

While peanut butter was a hit at the fair, the first peanut butter spreads were not the creamy, long-lasting treat that we know today. This was because peanut butter was packed in barrels, not in sealed jars. In barrels, the peanut butter would spoil very quickly. In fact, one peanut butter company in Columbus, Ohio, refused to sell its product outside Ohio. The peanut butter might spoil during shipping to an out-of-state store.

In 1922, Joseph Rosefield began using a churn to make his peanut butter creamy. He also invented a new peanut butter formula. The oil would not separate from peanut butter made with this formula. Rosefield's peanut butter could be stored for up to a year. Peanut butter that was made this way is very similar to the spread we use today.

About half of all peanuts produced in the United States are used to make peanut butter and other peanut spreads. Years ago, peanut farmers would have had a hard time picking the number of peanuts needed to make millions of jars of peanut butter. Peanut picking was done with a horse-drawn machine that was operated by many people. It could only plow one row of peanuts at a time. Both planting and harvesting peanuts took a long time.

Workers planting peanuts by hand in the early 1900s

A farmer in Georgia digs up peanuts.

Today, a peanut-picking machine called a digger requires just one operator. It can plow up to eight rows of peanuts at a time.

What happens next to peanuts that will end up as peanut butter? First, the shells are removed. Then the peanuts are roasted, and the skins are taken off. The peanuts are ground, heated, and cooled. To make chunky peanut butter, peanut bits are added back to the creamy mixture. Finally, the peanut butter is packed in jars.

A Thought Before We Eat

While many people enjoy eating peanuts, others are **allergic** to them. They may become sick—or even die—from eating peanuts, peanut products, or foods that have touched peanuts. Smelling and touching peanut products can also cause an allergic reaction. People with a peanut allergy need to check food labels carefully.

A peanut allergy warning poster

No Nuts!

The symptoms of an allergic reaction to peanuts may include **hives**; swollen or itchy lips, eyes, or tongue; and difficulty breathing and swallowing. A person who has a peanut allergy might also feel dizzy or very tired after eating even a small amount of peanuts. The person may also have a rapid heartbeat or chills.

The treatment for an allergic reaction to peanuts includes the use of a drug called epinephrine (eh-pih-NEF-rin). People who know they are allergic to peanuts may carry a needle filled with the drug to be injected in an emergency. Epinephrine works by helping the body open breathing passages. If someone you know has an allergic reaction to peanuts, he or she should get medical attention right away.

Doctors aren't sure exactly why some people have peanut allergies. They do know that peanuts are one of the foods to which people are most allergic. By being aware of the symptoms of peanut allergies, you could help save the life of someone you know.

Visit the Peanut Museum

In the 1840s, the first peanut crop was grown near a Virginia town called Waverly. Now Waverly is home to the first museum in the United States that is all about one of America's most important crops.

The First Peanut Museum was founded in 1990. Thousands of people visit it every year. It's a great place to see a bit of peanut history.

This working peanut picker from The First Peanut Museum separates the peanuts from the vines.

Inside and outside the museum, visitors can see some of the old tools that were developed to plant and harvest peanuts. Some of the machines on display, such as an old-fashioned peanut picker, are more than 120 years old.

The museum also has many photographs showing the earliest days of peanut production and **cultivation**. You can see curtains made from old peanut sacks and exhibits on the many different uses for the peanut. Of course, there is a display about George Washington Carver there, too. People living nearby have donated all of the items in the museum.

The one thing you won't find at the peanut museum is a peanut snack. You'll have to buy that at one of the many peanut stores near the museum.

One of the goals of the museum is to clear up myths about peanuts. Because of the peanut's name, many people believe that it's a nut. Other people believe that peanuts grow on trees!

These peanuts could be used as snacks—or might end up in a product such as shaving cream or ink.

Peanuts have come a long way since their beginnings in South America. Today, peanuts are one of the world's major food sources. Thanks to George Washington Carver, peanuts have many other uses, too. The next time you see a jar of peanut butter on a supermarket shelf, think of the amazing history of the little "goober."

Glossary

allergic having a reaction to a particular substance

climate the average weather conditions of a particular place or region

cultivation the preparation of land for raising crops

harvesting gathering a crop

hives raised, red patches on the skin as a result of an allergic reaction

imitation a copy of something else

legume a member of a large family of herbs, shrubs, and trees having fruits that are dry, single-celled pods, which split into two pieces when ripe

nitrogen a chemical element found in all living things

nutrients substances that provide needed vitamins and minerals to your body

pegs the budding parts of the peanut plant, which grow down away from the plant and into the soil

pollinated fertilized a plant by transferring pollen